AF207018

TEENS DEALING WITH
ONLINE BULLYING

by Muriel Knabb

BrightPoint Press

San Diego, CA

© 2025 BrightPoint Press
an imprint of ReferencePoint Press, Inc.
Printed in the United States

For more information, contact:
BrightPoint Press
PO Box 27779
San Diego, CA 92198
www.BrightPointPress.com

Content Consultant: Christopher Donoghue, PhD, Professor of Sociology, Montclair State University

LIBRARY OF CONGRESS CATALOGING-IN-PUBLICATION DATA

Name: Knabb, Muriel, author.
Title: Teens Dealing with Online Bullying / by Muriel Knabb.
Description: San Diego, CA: BrightPoint Press, Inc., 2025 | Series: Teens Dealing with Adversity | Audience: Grades 7–9 | Includes bibliographical references and index.
Identifiers: ISBN: 9781678208929 (hardcover) | ISBN: 9781678208936 (eBook)
The complete Library of Congress record is available at www.loc.gov.

CONTENTS

AT A GLANCE

- Online bullying is the repeated use of technology to intentionally harm victims. It is also called cyberbullying.

- Cyberbullying can happen anytime and anywhere. It is harder to escape than in-person bullying.

- Nearly half of teenagers aged 13 to 17 have experienced cyberbullying.

- Online bullying can hurt teenagers physically, emotionally, and mentally.

- It can be hard for teens to admit that they are being cyberbullied.

- Online bullying can affect teens socially and academically. These outward signs can help people tell if their loved ones are being cyberbullied.

- Practicing online safety can help teens avoid being cyberbullied.

- Teens experiencing cyberbullying should not respond to the bully. Instead, they should block the bully, screenshot the harassing material, and tell a trusted adult about the cyberbullying.

- School programs, online resources, and anti-bullying tools can help prevent bullying.

JAYLEN'S NIGHTMARE

Jaylen was using his computer to attend school virtually when his bully first appeared. Someone hacked into his school account. They changed his screen name to "Loser." Then, while he was using Zoom to do schoolwork, he started receiving threatening messages. The **harassment** got worse. Teachers started receiving rude messages from Jaylen's account.

Cyberbullying can happen to children, teens, and adults.

Some people call suicides linked to cyberbullying *cyberbullicides*.

Jaylen's mother watched the online bullying spiral out of control. She reported the harassment to the school. But the cyberbullying continued.

Jaylen changed schools. He was hoping that would stop the harassment. But it was not long before another message popped up on his screen. "im still here haha," it taunted. The bully had found him.

The bullying spread beyond his school accounts. Threatening messages appeared on Jaylen's PlayStation. Fake 911 calls were made from his home phone. The bully began encouraging Jaylen to hurt himself. One message said, "If you promise to kill yourself, I'll stop." Jaylen considered it. He just wanted to be left alone.

Jaylen's mother did everything she could to protect her son. She reported the bullying to Jaylen's new school. She told the family's internet provider. She even contacted the police. But the bully remained hidden.

The abuse went on for 10 months. But one day, Jaylen's nightmare came to an

Cyberbullying is a crime in many states.

abrupt end. His bully sent him a message. It said that the bully's mother had learned about the online harassment. The bully apologized and disappeared.

ONLINE BULLYING

Jaylen is far from the only teenager to be a victim of online bullying. For some teens, the consequences can be deadly. Online bullying can make teenagers feel helpless and alone. But they do not have to suffer in silence. When teens reach out for help, they can learn to fight against online bullying.

CHAPTER ONE

WHAT IS ONLINE BULLYING?

Bullying is when a person or a group causes harm to others who hold less power than they do. Power does not always mean physical strength. It can also come from popularity. It can come from being older than someone else. Some people may have less power than others simply because they are new to a school. They may have less power if they are different from others in some way.

Verbal harassment is the most common form of bullying.

Most cyberbullying is done by a person's classmates.

Bullying has always been around. But technology created a new way to harass people. It allows bullying to take place online. This is also called cyberbullying. Cyberbullying is the repeated use of technology to intentionally harm others. People can send hurtful messages through texts or social media. They can threaten physical violence. They can spread rumors to their peers. They may even send sexual images.

Technology did not just create new ways to hurt people. It also made bullying harder to escape. Online bullying can happen at any time and in any place. "Social media doesn't turn off," says Joan Luby. Luby is a child psychologist. "It's 24/7."[1]

Cyberbullying victims face other challenges too. Their bully may be unknown. This makes it hard to stop the harassment. Mean posts may also reach a larger audience than face-to-face bullying. This can shame victims in front of hundreds or even thousands of people.

Bullies might also be more cruel online than they would be in person. Eric Alcera is a doctor. He specializes in child psychology.

Two-thirds of young people who experienced cyberbullying said that the harassment had a negative impact on how they felt about themselves.

He says, "People will do and say hurtful or [mean] things online that they would never say in person."[2]

HOW COMMON IS ONLINE BULLYING?

The internet is an everyday part of teenagers' lives. In 2022, a study found that 97 percent of teens use the internet every day. About 95 percent have access to a smartphone. Around 90 percent have access to a computer. Of the teens surveyed, 46 percent say they use the internet almost constantly. This is an increase from 2015.

As access to technology has grown, so has cyberbullying. In 2022, a study found that 46 percent of teenagers aged 13 to 17 had experienced cyberbullying. Girls aged 15 to 17 are the most likely to experience cyberbullying. But online bullying can happen to anyone.

Other characteristics can also make students more likely to be cyberbullied. More than 70 percent of teens with disabilities reported being cyberbullied. Gay and bisexual teens are more than twice as likely to be cyberbullied than their peers. And transgender teens are more likely to be cyberbullied than **cisgender** teens. Race can also be a factor. More than 20 percent of Black teens and 11 percent of Hispanic teens report being cyberbullied due to their race.

More than 50 percent of teens say that online bullying is a major problem.

TYPES OF CYBERBULLYING

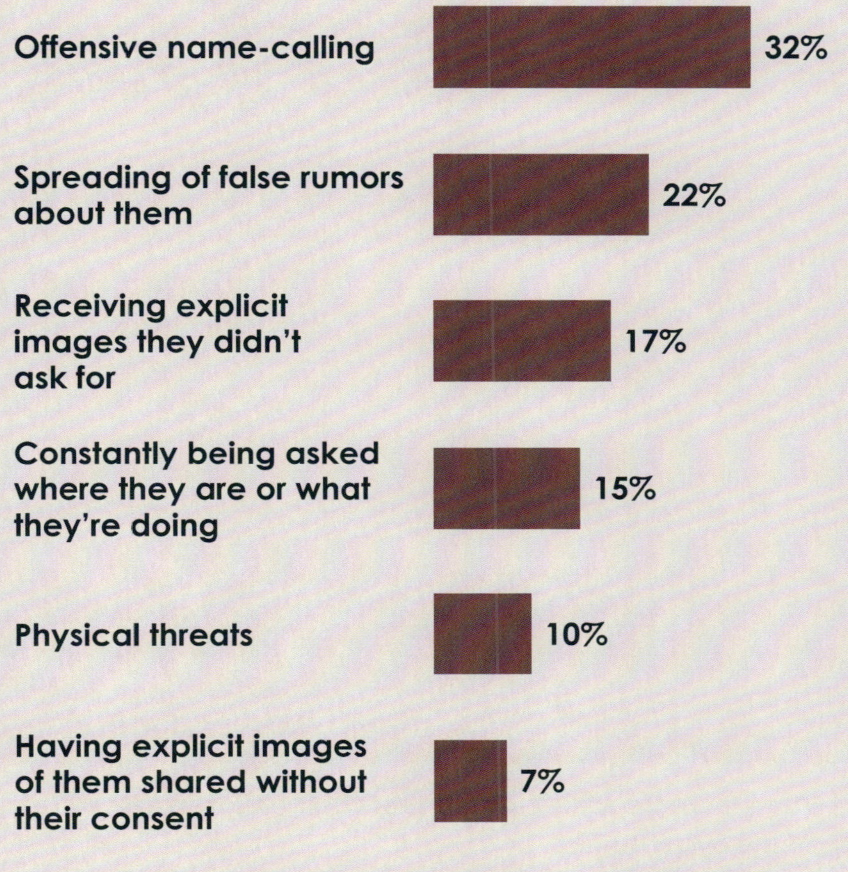

Source: Emily A. Vogels, "Teens and Cyberbullying 2022," Pew Research Center, *December 15, 2022.* www.pewresearch.org.

In 2022, the Pew Research Center asked teens about what types of cyberbullying they had experienced.

Many teachers agree. Stacey Dammann works at the York College of Pennsylvania. She says, "Cyberbullying is the most

Many parents aren't aware that their children are being cyberbullied.

concerning form of bullying. It has become increasingly more **prevalent** in schools."[3]

But online bullying does not happen only in schools. Some teens are bullied by strangers. They may be harassed on social media. They might be bullied in online

video games. Online bullying can creep into
every area of a person's internet life.

THE MANY FACES OF ONLINE BULLYING

Online bullying can take many different
forms. In Francesca's case, it took the form
of sexual harassment. Francesca lives in
New Jersey. She was 14 years old when
she was called into the principal's office.
The principal told her that a classmate had
used **artificial intelligence** (AI) to create
nude images of her.

The student had found a real image of
Francesca. He then used an AI website
to turn the photo into a nude image.
He had done this with images of more
than thirty female students. The student

then sent the images to other classmates on Snapchat.

"I just started crying because I didn't know what to do," says Francesca. "I didn't think this could happen to me."[4] Other classmates were experiencing similar feelings. They said they felt humiliated and powerless.

Caitlyn was also a teenage victim of cyberbullying. Her friends began bullying her at school. Soon the abuse moved online. The people she had thought were her friends started sending her horrible text messages. They called her hurtful names on social media. They said she was ugly. Some even told her she should kill herself. "You start thinking, 'Maybe they are right,'" Caitlyn said in a television interview, starting to cry. "'Maybe this is my fault.'"[5]

Tom was bullied for being gay. His bullies harassed him over Facebook and in texts. They created fake profiles to send him messages. The messages told him to kill himself. Tom thinks the people who sent the messages were harassing him for entertainment. But the bullying hurt him. "I would lie in my bed and just cry," Tom says. "It kind of destroys you."[6] He admits that he

Cyberbullying occurs on every major social media platform.

used to fall asleep hoping that he would not wake up.

WHY DOES ONLINE BULLYING HAPPEN?

Fifteen percent of teens admit to cyberbullying. People bully others for

many reasons. Sometimes it is because
they think it will make them popular. They
may think cyberbullying is entertaining. One
study found that 81 percent of teens believe
that people cyberbully because they think
online bullying is funny. They may not know
the severe consequences their actions
can have.

Others know that cyberbullying is wrong.
But they may do it anyway. Some teens use
bullying to cope with their own emotions.
They may have negative home lives. Others
may be victims of bullying themselves. This
does not make their actions okay. But it can
help explain why they hurt others.

One journalist interviewed a teenager
named James. James used to
cyberbully his classmates. He sent them

mean messages. He says he started cyberbullying because he was bored. But he quickly began using online bullying as an outlet for his anger.

"I found myself releasing my own personal anger through abusing other people **anonymously**," James says. "The feeling of not having to worry about people knowing who you are is powerful and addictive. I found myself resorting to abusing others when I was bored, upset, lonely, or angry. It made me feel like I was important and influential in people's lives, even though what I was prompting them to do was negative."[7]

Cyberbullying may also be attractive because it is easy to quickly send mean messages. The people behind

Some people are pressured to cyberbully by their peers.

the messages do not have to be strong.
They do not even have to know their
victims. Being anonymous may also make
cyberbullies less afraid of getting caught.
In addition, online bullying allows people
to hurt others without seeing the effect the
bullying has on the victims. This might let
them feel less bad about their actions.

CHAPTER TWO

HOW ONLINE BULLYING AFFECTS TEENS

Online bullying hurts teens in many ways. Some teens are hurt physically by the stress of the harassment. Stress can cause physical problems. Teens may lose their appetites. Others may overeat and gain weight. Some may have trouble sleeping. Others may sleep too much. Some experience headaches or stomachaches.

Cyberbullying also often hurts teens emotionally. One study found that

Online bullying can make people feel hurt, angry, and scared.

Young people who experience cyberbullying may be at an increased risk for eating disorders.

93 percent of cyberbullying victims reported negative mental health effects. Some victims develop mental illnesses. This includes anxiety and depression. Others may develop eating disorders. Some even experience **PTSD** from the bullying.

Cyberbullying can also cause other effects. Some people begin using drugs to cope with the abuse. Others hurt themselves. Young people who are cyberbullied are twice as likely to self-harm as their peers. They are more than four times as likely to have thoughts of suicide. Some act on these thoughts. Victims of cyberbullying are twice as likely to attempt suicide as their peers. People with thoughts of self-harm or suicide should speak to a trusted adult or therapist immediately.

OUTWARD SIGNS OF CYBERBULLYING

Unfortunately, physical and emotional effects can be hard to see. And many teens do not tell people that they are being cyberbullied. "Being bullied may be one of the hardest things for children to discuss with parents," says Dr. Alcera. "The topic alone may be embarrassing for them or something they don't want to admit."[8] Teens may also be afraid of what the bullies will do if they report the abuse. Others who are bullied may be afraid of getting in trouble themselves. But there are some outward signs that concerned friends and family can look for.

Teens who are being bullied often start struggling in school. Their grades

Cyberbullying can cause students to dislike school.

might suffer. The students might drop out of clubs or sports. They may start skipping school. A 2022 study found that two-thirds of cyberbullying victims said that their bullying made it hard for them to learn or feel safe at school.

People can also look for social changes. Teens experiencing cyberbullying may appear anxious or sad. They may be quieter than usual. Some start spending more time on their phones or computers. They might avoid their friends. Their peers might be mean or rude toward them. These can all be signs of cyberbullying.

THE MANY EFFECTS OF CYBERBULLYING

Francesca told her mom that fake nude images had been shared of her and her classmates. Her mom was shocked. She reached out to the school. The school assured her that the images were gone. They said that Snapchat images disappear. But Francesca's mom knew that they could have been screenshotted. The images could have been saved elsewhere.

Teens have developed several ways to save supposedly private Snapchat photos.

She was also upset when she learned how little the school punished the student who had made the images.

"[The school] is not listening to the girls who have been victimized," Francesca's mom told the news. "[The victims] feel uncomfortable. They feel traumatized. They feel hurt. They feel betrayed. And nobody listens to them."[9]

Unfortunately, there was little that Francesca or her mom could do. AI technology is progressing faster than laws are. Very few states have laws about making AI images. "I felt sad and helpless at the lack of **legislation** and school AI policies to protect me," Francesca says.[10]

Caitlyn did not tell her parents about the harassment she was suffering. She tried to handle it on her own. But the bullying did not stop. "I ended up with anxiety [and] depression," she revealed later. "I had **panic attacks** all the time."[11] Her abuse continued for 2 years.

Tom was similarly affected. The person who bullied him kept telling Tom to kill himself. Tom started considering it.

Social Media Mayhem

In 2022, 10,000 teens were surveyed about their experiences with cyberbullying. The study asked teens which social media platforms they had been using when they were cyberbullied. Instagram was identified as the platform most commonly used by cyberbullies. Facebook was the second-most used platform. Snapchat was the third.

CHAPTER THREE

FINDING SUPPORT

When a teen is being cyberbullied, it may feel as if there is no hope. But there are people who can help. There are resources available to help teens fight back against cyberbullying.

Some resources are aimed at preventing online bullying. Others support teens who have gone through cyberbullying. All can help teens fight online bullying.

Telling an adult about cyberbullying isn't tattling—it's standing up to harassment.

STAYING SAFE ONLINE

It is never a victim's fault for being cyberbullied. But there are ways to prevent online bullying. One way to prevent it is to practice being safe online.

Many social media platforms have tools to protect users. These tools include privacy settings. On platforms such as Instagram and TikTok, teens can control who is allowed to view their accounts. They can make their accounts private. This lets only their friends view their content. This can make it more difficult for bullies to send hurtful messages. It can also prevent stalking. Stalking involves the repeated unwanted following or harassing of another person. Stalking can be in person or online. Online stalkers may message

Private accounts allow users to decide who can see and interact with their content.

people persistently. They might make fake accounts to avoid being blocked.

Teens should also keep their personal information private. They should never post their address or phone number on social media. This can prevent people from harassing them over the phone. It can also stop people from finding them in person.

People experiencing cyberbullying should block the phone numbers, email addresses, and social media accounts of their harassers.

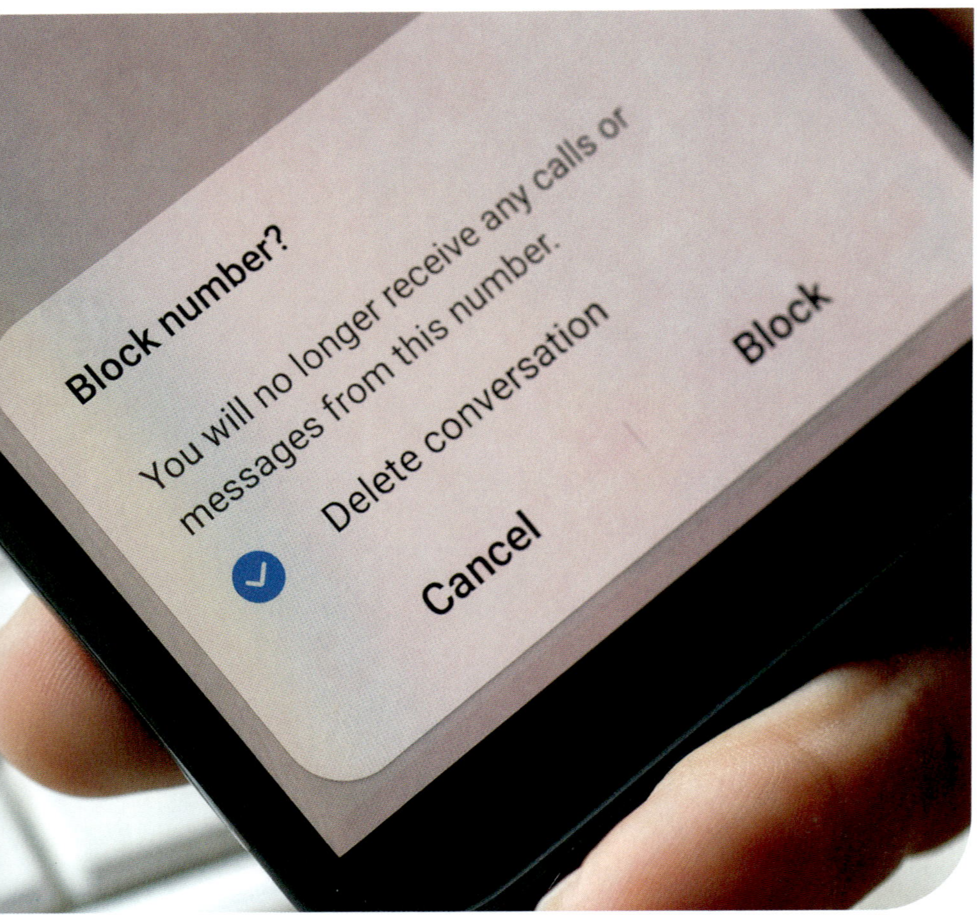

Another way to stay safe online is to keep passwords secret. Teens should not share their passwords with anyone. This includes close friends. Sharing passwords can allow people to hack into their accounts.

WHEN CYBERBULLYING HAPPENS

Even teens who take steps to stay safe online may encounter cyberbullying. It is important for people in this situation to know what to do next. For example, if a teen sees a harassing message or post, they should not respond to the bullying. They should instead take a screenshot of the material. Then they should block the harassing user. If the post is on a social media platform, they should report it. Social media websites often have instructions that show users how to report content and users. A trusted adult may also be able to help a teen report online bullying.

Next, the teen should show the screenshot to a trusted adult. This could be a parent. It could also be a teacher. They can help the teen figure out the next steps to take. The adult may contact the cyberbully's parents. They may also report

Speaking Up

Reaching out for help can be hard. Only 10 percent of teens who are cyberbullied tell a trusted adult about the abuse. Teens who are afraid to speak up can report the bullying anonymously. Online anti-bullying organizations provide confidential cyberbullying tip lines. Some schools also have ways to anonymously report bullying.

the post to the cyberbully's principal. If the
post is threatening or sexually explicit, they
may even report it to the police.

DEALING WITH ONLINE BULLYING

Online bullying can make teens feel
powerless. It can worsen mental health
problems. But there are people who can
help teens deal with this bullying. These
people can help resolve online conflicts.
They can also help teens process the
emotions that come with cyberbullying.

School counselors can help teens who
are dealing with online bullying. So can
teachers and principals. These people
can take action against students who
are cyberbullying. They can also counsel
cyberbullying victims.

Sometimes teens need more help than schools offer. These teens can find therapists. Therapists are trained to help teens who are going through difficult situations. They can also help people who are suffering from mental illnesses. School counselors can connect teens with therapists. So can doctors. Parents can help teens find support too.

Once a teen has found a therapist, they can begin therapy. There are many different types of therapy. Teens may talk to a therapist one-on-one. They may attend therapy with a group of teens going through similar challenges. One of the most common types of therapy is cognitive behavioral therapy (CBT). In this type of therapy, therapists work to help people

About 8 million teens in the United States receive mental health treatment each year.

change negative thoughts and emotions. This can be helpful for teens dealing with the effects of bullying.

Teens can also find help online. They can reach out to an anti-bullying organization. Some organizations have trained counselors who can talk to teens online. They can give teens advice about how to deal with cyberbullying. They can also connect teens to other resources. Many of these organizations have information about preventing cyberbullying. This information includes articles and videos. Some organizations even train students to act as peer counselors. These students can then help their classmates fight cyberbullying.

Sometimes victims of cyberbullying need the help of law enforcement. Police may get involved for a number of reasons. They can help teens if a cyberbully is stalking them. They can also help people who are being sexually harassed. This includes people who have been sent sexually explicit images. It also includes people who have had their own private images sent to other people.

In some states, cyberbullying is a crime. Police are better able to help cyberbullying victims in these states. In California, people found guilty of cyberbullying may face jail time. They might also be required to pay a fine.

Digital forensic investigators can find deleted data on phones and computers. This can help police collect evidence of cybercrimes.

PREVENTING ONLINE BULLYING

Online bullying can never be fully prevented. But there are ways to reduce it. This starts with teaching teens to be respectful online. There are several ways to do this. One way is by educating teens about cyberbullying. Some anti-bullying organizations have speakers. They talk to students at schools across the country. They tell students about the effects of cyberbullying. They tell them how to prevent it. They also explain how to deal with it when it happens.

School anti-bullying programs are another way to prevent bullying. These programs begin with creating anti-bullying policies. The policies should include rules against both in-person bullying and cyberbullying. Students should be taught

these rules. They should also learn how to

intervene when they see bullying happening.

In addition, they should be taught how

to report bullying. These policies help

students prevent bullying and stop it when it

is happening.

In 2022, Trisha Prabhu published a book about being responsible online.

Specialized tools can also help teens prevent cyberbullying. One of these tools is ReThink. ReThink is an app created by Trisha Prabhu. She invented the software when she was just 13 years old. Trisha was horrified by the stories of cyberbullied teens dying by suicide. She wanted to do something to stop these deaths. Her app seeks to stop cyberbullying at the source. ReThink analyzes the messages that teens type. It warns users when they are about to send something that might be mean. Teens can still send the message. But many choose to change their language. In early tests, ReThink reduced the number of mean messages sent by teens by 93 percent.

COPING WITH ONLINE BULLYING

Sometimes cyberbullying victims can use their experiences to help others. Francesca decided to share her story. She began advocating for a nationwide law that would make sharing fake sexual images illegal. "No kid, teen, or woman should ever have to experience what I went through," she says.[12]

Two-thirds of young people have helped someone who was being bullied online.

She says that advocating for new laws to help other potential victims makes her feel empowered.

"Getting through cyberbullying was the hardest thing I've ever had to go through," Caitlyn says. It got easier when she reached out for help. She suffered in silence for years. But she finally told her mom that she was being bullied. Her mom helped her get therapy.

"As soon as I told someone what was actually going on, everything changed," she says. She was able to get the help she needed. She uses her experience to educate other people about cyberbullying. "Now I'm able to help other people going through cyberbullying as well."[13]

Tom moved to a new school to escape his bullies. He then decided to speak out against bullying. He became an anti-bullying ambassador for the Diana Award Anti-Bullying Programme. This organization raises awareness about bullying. It also helps teachers and students learn to prevent bullying. Tom and his classmates made a movie about the effects of bullying. It was shown in theaters across Great Britain.

Cyberbullies can change too. Once James realized how hurtful cyberbullying can be, he deleted the account he was using to harass people. He also apologized to the people he had hurt. His confession made him feel better. He says he feels as if a weight has been removed from his life.

People can avoid cyberbullying by spending less time online.

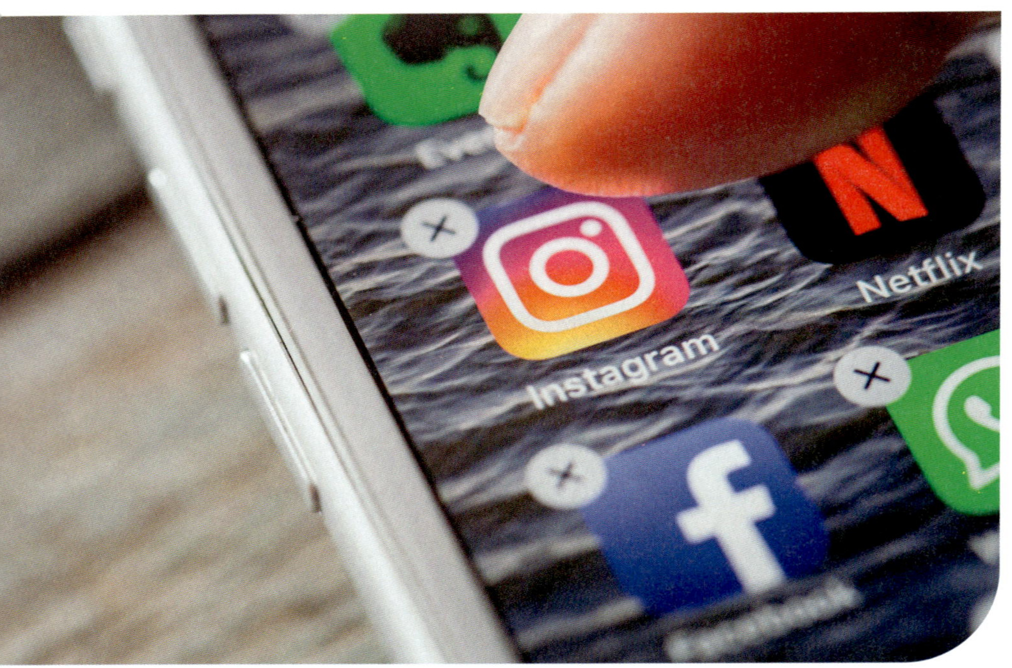

He offered advice to other teens who might want to cyberbully. James says, "My advice to the internet trolls and bullies is to deactivate your account before things get out of hand. If you feel depressed or upset, and begin to turn to bullying, or are being bullied, I strongly advise you to talk to an adult."[14]

Online bullying can seem impossible to deal with. But teens do not have to shoulder the burden alone. Both cyberbullies and their victims can find help. With the proper resources and support, people can learn to cope with online bullying.

GLOSSARY

anonymously

without people knowing who someone is

artificial intelligence

computer programs capable of doing complicated tasks such as creating images

cisgender

identifying with the same gender one was assigned at birth

harassment

continuously bothering, intimidating, or bullying someone

legislation

laws

panic attacks

sudden feelings of intense anxiety even when there is no threat

prevalent

happening often

PTSD

post-traumatic stress disorder, a mental disorder caused by a scary or dangerous event that can cause flashbacks, anxiety, depression, and physical pain

SOURCE NOTES

CHAPTER ONE: WHAT IS ONLINE BULLYING?

1. Quoted in Mary Elizabeth Gillis, "Cyberbullying on Rise in US," *Fox News*, September 21, 2019. www.foxnews.com.

2. Quoted in "What Are the Effects of Cyberbullying?" *Hackensack Meridian Health*, August 17, 2020. www.hackensackmeridianhealth.org.

3. Quoted in Liz Regalia, "Do Schools Do Enough to Prevent Bullying?" *Care*, August 31, 2023. www.care.com.

4. Quoted in Kristine Parks, "New Jersey High School Girls 'Humiliated' After Classmates Use AI to Generate Fake Nude Images," *Fox News*, November 2, 2023. www.foxnews.com.

5. Quoted in "Cyberbullying," *YouTube*, uploaded by Dr. Phil, February 12, 2020. www.youtube.com.

6. Quoted in "#StandUpToBullying," *YouTube*, uploaded by AntiBullyingPro, May 25, 2017. www.youtube.com.

7. Quoted in Elizabeth Soal, "Confessions of a Cyberbully," *NetDoctor*, February 3, 2014. www.netdoctor.co.uk.

CHAPTER TWO: HOW ONLINE BULLYING AFFECTS TEENS

8. Quoted in "What Are the Effects of Cyberbullying?"

9. Quoted in Parks, "New Jersey High School Girls 'Humiliated' After Classmates Use AI to Generate Fake Nude Images."

10. Quoted in "Victim of Deepfake Porn at NJ High School Pushes for Federal Law Targeting AI-Generated Explicit Content," *NBC New York*, January 18, 2024. www.nbcnewyork.com.

11. Quoted in "Cyberbullying."

CHAPTER THREE: FINDING SUPPORT

12. Quoted in "Victim of Deepfake Porn at NJ High School Pushes for Federal Law Targeting AI-Generated Explicit Content."

13. Quoted in "Cyberbullying."

14. Quoted in Soal, "Confessions of a Cyberbully."

BOOKS

C.R. McKay, *I Am Being Cyberbullied . . . What's Next?* New York: Rosen Publishing Group, 2021.

Marie-Thérèse Miller, PhD, *Teens and Cyberbullying*. San Diego, CA: ReferencePoint Press, 2021.

Jill C. Wheeler, *Reach Out: Tips for Helping Someone in Crisis*. San Diego, CA: ReferencePoint Press, 2024.

INTERNET SOURCES

Angelica Bottaro, "Cyberbullying," *VeryWell Health*, October 6, 2023. www.verywellhealth.com.

"Cyberbullying: What Is It and How to Stop It," *UNICEF*, February 2024. www.unicef.org.

"What Is Cyberbullying?" *Nemour Teens Health*, n.d. https://kidshealth.org.

WEBSITES

Cyberbullying Research Center
www.cyberbullying.org

The Cyberbullying Research Center website was launched in 2005. It is dedicated to providing information about the causes and consequences of cyberbullying. Its website also contains firsthand accounts of cyberbullying.

PACER Center's Teens Against Bullying
www.pacerteensagainstbullying.org

PACER Center is an organization that helps children with disabilities. The center's Teens Against Bullying site gives teens information about preventing and coping with bullying. It also contains stories from teens who have experienced bullying.

Stopbullying.gov
www.stopbullying.gov

Stopbullying.gov is a government website dedicated to preventing and stopping bullying. The site has a section devoted to understanding and handling cyberbullying.

INDEX

IMAGE CREDITS

Cover: © Motortion/iStockphoto

5: © chainarong06/Shutterstock Images

7: © myboys.me/Shutterstock Images

8: © Daisy Daisy/Shutterstock Images

10: © kali9/iStockphoto

13: © FatCamera/iStockphoto

14: © Motortion Films/Shutterstock Images

16: © TheVisualsYouNeed/Shutterstock Images

19: © Red Line Editorial

20: © Olimpik/Shutterstock Images

24: © Primakov/Shutterstock Images

27: © GCShutter/iStockphoto

29: © Motortion/iStockphoto

30: © SpeedKingz/Shutterstock Images

33: © sebra/Shutterstock Images

35: © Alberto Menendez Cervero/Shutterstock Images

39: © digitalskillet/Shutterstock Images

41: © Kaspars Grinvalds/Shutterstock Images

42: © wisely/Shutterstock Images

47: © SeventyFour/Shutterstock Images

49: © microgen/iStockphoto

51: © Monkey Business Images/Shutterstock Images

52: © Marvin Lynchard/Department of Defense

54: © Prostock-Studio/Shutterstock Images

56: © Michael Jay Berlin/Shutterstock Images

ABOUT THE AUTHOR

Muriel Knabb, MEd, served as a classroom teacher, assistant principal, and principal in elementary schools for more than 30 years. She investigated many incidents of in-person bullying and cyberbullying in her job as a school principal. She worked with students, parents, and staff to create a positive, safe school climate. Today, she writes fiction and nonfiction for young people.